What

eople

Do

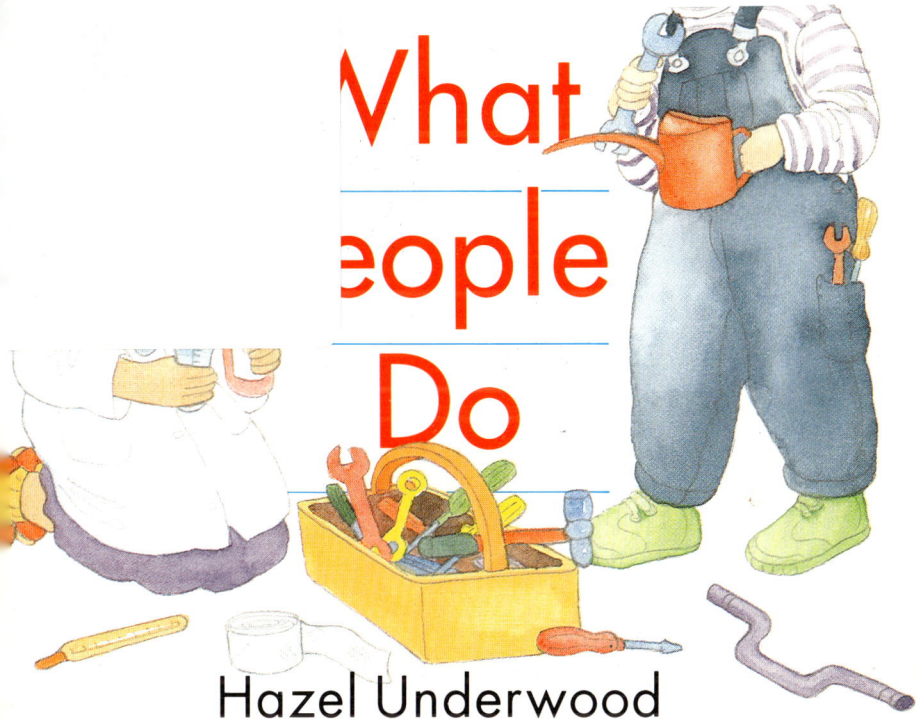

Hazel Underwood

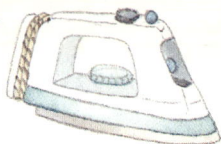

People do all kinds of jobs.
Some people work at home.

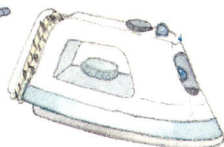

5

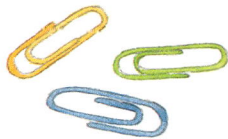

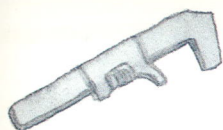

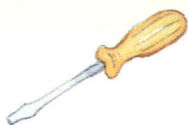

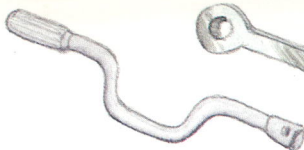

What job would you like
to do?
Would you like to work in
a garage?

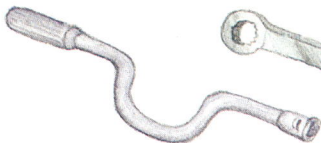

My car needs some oil.

9

Would you like to be a gardener?

These flowers need some water.

11

Would you like to be a police officer?

You're driving too fast!

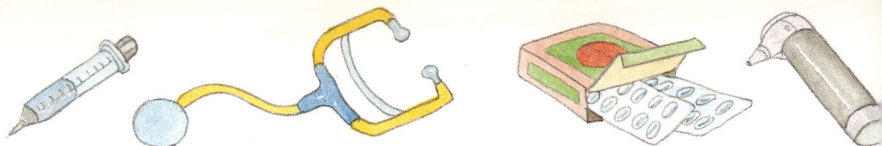

Would you like to be a doctor?

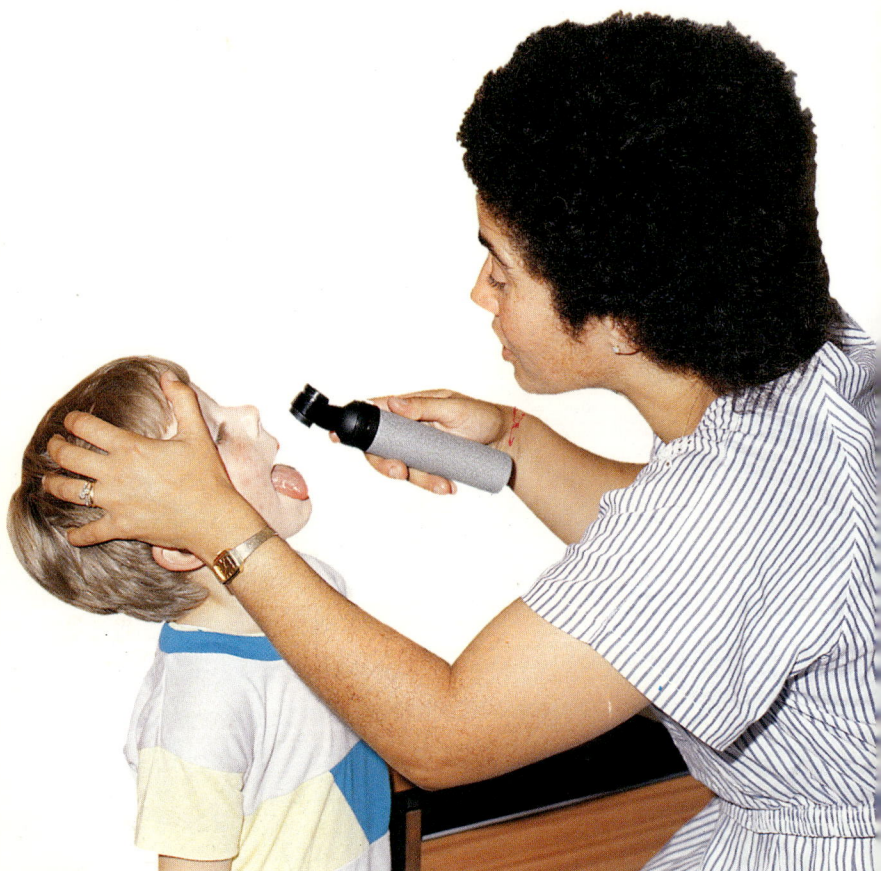

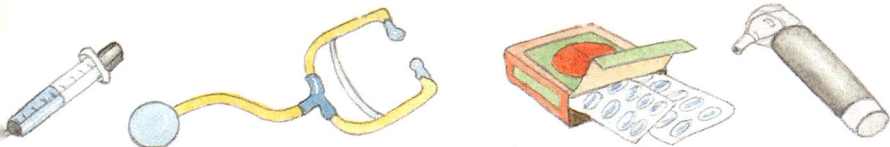

How are you today?

15

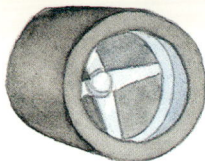

Would you like to be a racing driver?

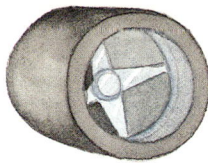

I'm driving very fast.

17

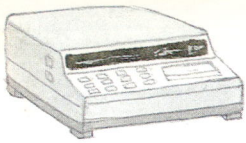

Would you like to work
in a shop?

I'm counting all the money.

19

Would you like to be
a pop star?

I'm singing and dancing.

21

Would you like to be a farmer?

I'm feeding the
chickens.

23

Would you like to be a builder?

I'm building a block of flats.

25

Would you like to be a chef?

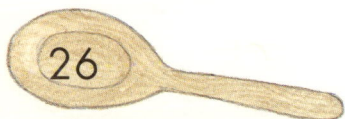

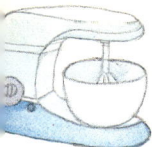

I'm making a cake.

27

There are hundreds of
different jobs.

Goodbye!

29

Can you think which people would need these tools for their jobs?

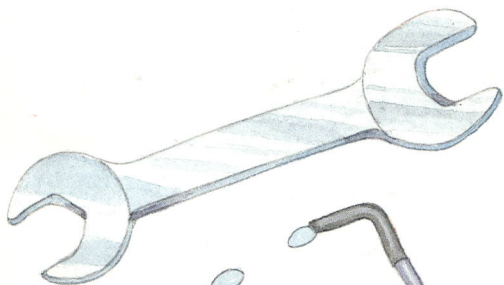

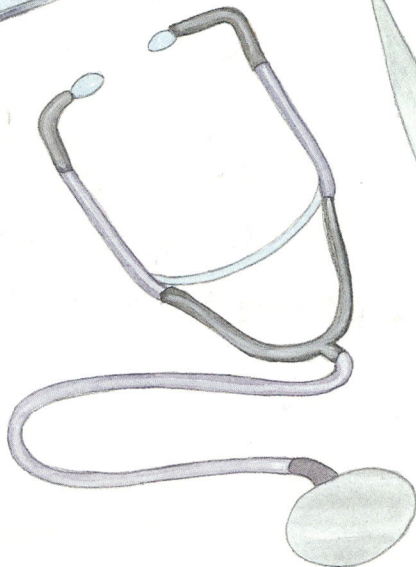